THE COMPLETE PIANO PLAYER
BEATLES
Arranged by Kenneth Baker

Wise Publications
London / New York / Sydney

Exclusive distributors:
Music Sales Limited
8/9 Frith Street, London W1V 5TZ, England.
Music Sales Pty Limited
120 Rothschild Avenue, Rosebery, NSW 2018, Australia.

This book © Copyright 1990 by
Wise Publications
Order No. NO18806
UK ISBN 0.7119.2281.0

Designed by Pearce Marchbank Studio
Arranged by Kenneth Baker
Compiled by Peter Evans
Music processed by Musicprint

Music Sales' complete catalogue lists thousands of
titles and is free from your local music shop, or direct from
Music Sales Limited. Please send £1.50 in stamps for postage to
Music Sales Limited, 8/9 Frith Street, London W1V 5TZ.

Printed in England by
J.B. Offset Printers (Marks Tey) Limited, Marks Tey, Essex

MICHELLE

Words & Music by John Lennon & Paul McCartney

I WANNA BE YOUR MAN

Words & Music by John Lennon & Paul McCartney

BLACKBIRD

Words & Music by John Lennon & Paul McCartney

IF I FELL

Words & Music by John Lennon & Paul McCartney

TICKET TO RIDE

Words & Music by John Lennon & Paul McCartney

13

WE CAN WORK IT OUT

Words & Music by John Lennon & Paul McCartney

Think of what I'm say - ing, we can work it out and get it straight, or say good-night.

We can work it out, ___ we can work it out. ___

Life is ver - y short ___
I have al - ways thought

___ and there's no time ___ for fuss - ing and
___ that it's a crime, ___ so I will

1.
fight - ing, my friend. ___

2.
ask you once a -

D.C. al Coda ⊕ *CODA*

gain.

15

STRAWBERRY FIELDS FOREVER

Words & Music by John Lennon & Paul McCartney

17

CARRY THAT WEIGHT

Words & Music by John Lennon & Paul McCartney

FROM ME TO YOU

Words & Music by John Lennon & Paul McCartney

WHEN I'M SIXTY FOUR

Words & Music by John Lennon & Paul McCartney

LUCY IN THE SKY WITH DIAMONDS

Words & Music by John Lennon & Paul McCartney

VERSES

Pic - ture your - self in a boat on a ri - ver, with
Fol - low her down to a bridge by a foun - tain, where

tan - ger - ine trees, and mar - ma - lade skies. Some - bo - dy calls you, you
rock - ing horse people eat marsh - mal - low pies. Ev - 'ry - one smiles as you

ans - wer quite slow - ly, a girl with ka - lei - de - scope eyes. ____
drift past the flow - ers that grow so in - cre - di - bly high. ____

I WANT TO HOLD YOUR HAND

Words & Music by John Lennon & Paul McCartney

D.S. al Coda

CODA

PAPERBACK WRITER

Words & Music by John Lennon & Paul McCartney

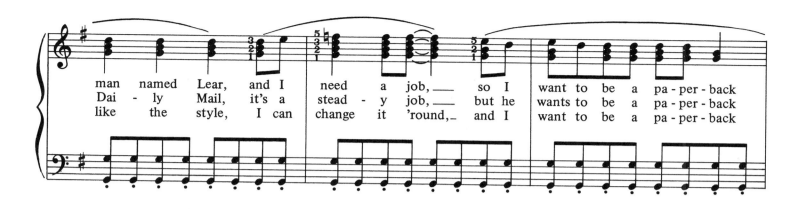

man named Lear, and I need a job, ___ so I want to be a pa-per-back
Dai - ly Mail, it's a stead - y job, ___ but he wants to be a pa-per-back
like the style, I can change it 'round, ___ and I want to be a pa-per-back

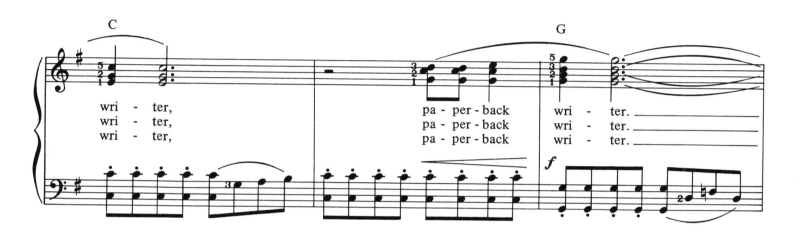

C   G

wri - ter,
wri - ter,   pa - per - back   wri - ter. ___
wri - ter,   pa - per - back   wri - ter. ___
                                        pa - per - back   wri - ter. ___

f

1.   2,3.
                                        D.C. 2nd time
                                        straight on 3rd time

                    2. It's a   Pa - per - back

mf   *mf*

P   P

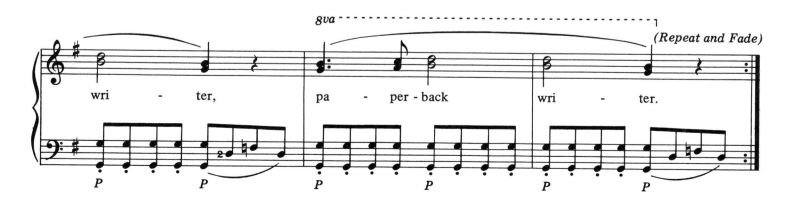

8va -

(Repeat and Fade)

wri - ter,   pa - per - back   wri - ter.

P   P   P   P   P   P

LOVELY RITA

Words & Music by John Lennon & Paul McCartney

31

GIRL

Words & Music by John Lennon & Paul McCartney

YOU'VE GOT TO HIDE YOUR LOVE AWAY

Words & Music by John Lennon & Paul McCartney

HEY JUDE

Words & Music by John Lennon & Paul McCartney

A DAY IN THE LIFE

Words & Music by John Lennon & Paul McCartney

Hav-ing read the book. I'd

love to turn _____ you _____ on.

cresc.

Woke up, got out of bed, dragged a comb a-cross my head.__ Found my
coat and grabbed my hat, made the bus in sec-onds flat.__ Found my

way down stairs and drank a cup, and look-ing up I no-ticed I was late. Found my
way up stairs and had a smoke, and somebod-y spoke, and I went in-to a dream.

D.C. al Coda

CODA

Now they know how ma-ny holes it takes to fill the Al-bert Hall, I'd

love to turn _____ you _____ on.

cresc.

39

HERE, THERE AND EVERYWHERE

Words & Music by John Lennon & Paul McCartney

SGT PEPPER'S LONELY HEARTS CLUB BAND

Words & Music by John Lennon & Paul McCartney

THIS BOY

Words & Music by John Lennon & Paul McCartney

45

I SAW HER STANDING THERE

Words & Music by John Lennon & Paul McCartney